Richard W. Hiley

The Inspiration of Scripture

An Examination into its Meaning, Origin and Theories Thereon

Richard W. Hiley

The Inspiration of Scripture
An Examination into its Meaning, Origin and Theories Thereon

ISBN/EAN: 9783337183394

Printed in Europe, USA, Canada, Australia, Japan

Cover: Foto ©Lupo / pixelio.de

More available books at **www.hansebooks.com**

AN EXAMINATION INTO ITS MEANING, ORIGIN

AND THEORIES THEREON

BY THE

REV. RICHARD W. HILEY, D.D.

VICAR OF WIGHILL, YORKSHIRE

' I believe in the Holy Ghost, who spake by the Prophets '

(Nicene Creed)

TO

A. S. FARRAR, D.D.

Canon Residentiary of Durham
&c.

FOR FORTY YEARS

MY COMPANION AND MINE OWN FAMILIAR FRIEND

I DEDICATE THESE PAGES

WITH AFFECTION AND RESPECT

PREFACE.

By the Statutes of the University of Oxford, the aspirant to the degree of D.D. is required to write dissertations on certain conditions. The following pages were primarily written for that purpose.

The subject is one that has occupied the writer's attention for many years, as has doubtless been the case with many men in holy orders. Of late years the inspiration of the Holy Scriptures has been much discussed. This may be attributed to the revived activity of the Church, to the increased and minute criticism expended on Scripture, and to the extended researches, historical and philological, which have marked the last half-century. Activity from within always provokes activity from without, and the assaults of scepticism have ever been co-ordinate with the zeal of believers. The inspiration of Scripture has been in this way assailed, denied, or explained away.

The writer has been at some considerable pains in collecting information on the various views propounded, and he has been vain enough to think that the result may be of service to others. Divinity students, candidates for holy orders, and thoughtful readers may not be disposed to wade through every treatise for and against the tenet, but may be disposed to have a summary of them all. It is with that hope that the following pages are printed.

When a subject has been for years in a person's thoughts, he will have digested the results of others to such an extent that he becomes unconscious of their origin. However, a list of works is appended, the contents of which have been freely used and, it is hoped, freely acknowledged. It would be presumptuous indeed to lay claim to any great originality; the writer would therefore say, as Montesquieu says somewhere: 'I have gathered a nosegay of flowers, and mine is the string that ties them.'

Should this essay live to see a second edition, some of the chapters may be considerably expanded.

The following are the principal works consulted on the subject:—

1. The Inspiration of Scripture: its Nature and Proofs, by Professor Lee, of Dublin.
2. The Inspiration and Authority of Scripture, by Bishop Hinds.

3. Aids to Faith; edited by Archbishop Thomson, with an Article on Inspiration by Bishop Harold Browne.

4. The Inspiration of Scripture: Five Lectures by Bishop Wordsworth.

5. Plenary Inspiration, by Professor Gaussen, of Geneva.

6. The Theory of Inspiration, by Rev. J. Wilson, Headmaster of Clifton College.

7. Inspiration, by Bishop Wilson (Calcutta).

8. Inspiration: an Article in the Preface to Westcott's Introduction to the New Testament.

9. A Catholic's Views of Inspiration: an Article by Cardinal Manning.

10. A Rejoinder by the same to a Critique on the above Article.

11. Foundations, by Archdeacon Pollock, containing an Essay on Inspiration.

12. Elements of Theology, with a Chapter on Inspiration, by Bishop Tomline.

Besides various essays, articles, and sermons by various authors.

THORPARCH, YORKSHIRE:
July 1885.

CONTENTS.

CHAPTER I.

THE RECEPTION OF THE BIBLE.

CHAPTER II.

THE BIBLE'S ACCOUNT OF ITSELF.

CHAPTER III.

CHRIST'S TREATMENT OF THE OLD TESTAMENT.

CHAPTER IV.

TREATMENT OF THE OLD TESTAMENT BY THE APOSTLES.

CHAPTER V.

ORIGIN OF THE NEW TESTAMENT.

CHAPTER VI.

MODUS OPERANDI OF INSPIRATION.

CHAPTER VII.

PHENOMENA SHOWN BY THE θεόπνευστος.

CHAPTER VIII.

THEORIES AS TO THE EXTENT OF THE INSPIRING INFLUENCE ON THE RECIPIENT.

CHAPTER IX.

EXAMINATION OF THE ABOVE THEORIES.

CHAPTER X.

EXAMINATION OF THEORIES (*continued*).

PAGE

CHAPTER XI.

SOME OBJECTIONS.

CHAPTER XII.

INSPIRATION TO BE EXPECTED.

THE
INSPIRATION OF SCRIPTURE.

CHAPTER I.

THE RECEPTION OF THE BIBLE.

Introduction—Peter and John at Beautiful Gate—Astonishment of multitude at the cure—Explanation—Same astonishment at the Bible—It exists—Cherished by Jews in spite of unpleasant contents—Then spread—Difference between Bible and Homer—Not for learned solely—Courts publicity, not fascination nor popularity—Has met constant opposition—Yet has wrought revolution—Same answer as Peter and John.

WE read in the Acts of the Apostles that when Peter and John went to the Temple to pray, at the usual hour, a well-known cripple, lying at the gate, solicited their alms. Peter replied, 'Silver and gold have I none, but . . . . in the name of Jesus Christ of Nazareth rise up and walk.' (Acts iii.) Immediately, we are told, the man's ankle-bones received strength, and he entered with them into the Temple, walking and leaping and praising God.

This marvellous restoration to health and vigour, of a cripple well-known for his affliction, created immense astonishment amongst the beholders. The story spread rapidly, like wildfire, and crowds came to see the wondrous cure, the recipient, and the agents.

On this, we are told that Peter soon explained the cure and its cause: ' Why look ye so earnestly on us, as though by our own power we had wrought this change. The God of our fathers has raised up His Son Jesus, and it is His name, through faith in His name, that hath made this man, whom ye see, whole.' As much as to say—had this cure been wrought by human power, it might well excite your wonder, but when we tell you that it is the power of God, you must cease to regard us as anything more than mere men, but men made instruments for the exhibition of a Divine power.

An astonishment something similar to the above might fill any impartial mind, on observing the history and the influence of the book called—the Bible.

We find in existence a book which wins its way into every country of the globe. In the earlier centuries of its history it was indeed confined mainly to one people, but the very veneration with which that one people regarded it, is not the least striking feature of its history. For, though it contains promises of countless blessings to them on certain conditions, it at the same time pours forth denunciations of fearful calamities if those conditions were unfulfilled. The nonfulfilment and the consequent calamities were frequent phases of their history, and yet in the midst of their most terrible sufferings, they clung tenaciously to the very books, the exponents of their misery.

After centuries of this exclusive tenure, by a change of dispensation, this book was allowed a wider range. The restriction was removed, and it was to be offered to every nation under the sun.

The extension has been slowly but certainly going on. Its advocates and supporters have translated it into language upon language, for the acceptance of nations of every blood and tongue.

The same might perhaps be said, to some extent, of the great writings of antiquity, whether Greek or Roman. The circulation of the poems of Homer has been immense, and as long as time shall run, they will enthral with fascination scholars of every nation, as powerfully as they held spell-bound the warriors who first heard them chanted at the banquets of the Ionian princes.

But there are wide differences between the circulation of the treasures of classic lore and that of the Bible.

These have been circulated in the main by men looking for some personal interest in the transaction. The copyist or the rhapsodist, the printer and the merchant, all looked for some personal return for their labour, however small. No such account can be given for the circulation of the Bible. It has ever been distributed, and is distributed still, with great labour and expense, and not unfrequently, *peril of life*. Its disseminators have often had nothing to gain and everything to lose by their efforts.

A still greater difference is this:—The other books referred to have appealed in the main to the *learned*. Homer and Cicero and Thucydides, as has been already said, have been and will be ever read by the lovers of learning of every land ; and in proportion to the amount of the intellectual culture of the recipients, so will be their appreciation of classical writings. But the audience, if the expression be allowable, is in each case limited, the range of operation circumscribed, the number influenced, though great in the aggregate, is small compared with the infinitely larger number to whom they are unknown.

That is not the case with the Bible. Though capable of occupying the mightiest intellects, and for their lifetime, and having, as a matter of fact, ranked the greatest minds amongst its servants, yet it has appealed and does appeal with affectionate yearning to the babes of mankind ; not to the mighty, not to the learned exclusively, but to the humblest and most down-trodden of men.

Even under the old dispensation, when limited to one people, a wide dissemination through that people was emphatically enjoined. · It was to be taught to their children, it was to be taught to their children's children, it was to be written on the door-posts of their houses, it was to be a frontlet between their eyes; it was to be the subject of their conversation whenever and wherever employed, so that it was their own fault if the whole of the sacred volumes were not known by heart, by every member of their commonwealth.

It may be said that at times exclusiveness in its circulation has been practised, but such exclusiveness has ever been considered a sign of corruption in the faith and practice of those of its professors. The Mahometan has his Koran and regards it with veneration, but to the mass of them it is a sealed book. The Roman Catholic holds to the Bible as tenaciously

as the Protestant, in many respects more so ; but he
considers it in practice to be treated like the phar-
maceutical materials of the physician, dangerous in
the hands of any one not specifically trained. The
founder of Mormonism alleged, as the authority for
his mission, golden plates received from heaven
with his revelation engraved thereon, but no one
ever saw them. This reservation is not the real
spirit of the Bible. It says to its recipients, 'Search
me,' and the spirit that it fosters is 'a meditation
therein day and night.'

And yet there is nothing in the style and contents of the Bible that can be said to be contrived
for *fascination*. It possesses, indeed, poetry and
imagery of surpassing beauty when rightly appre-
ciated, but poetical charm in the bulk of the
narrative is conspicuous by its absence, the style
is artless, the narrative devoid of meretricious orna-
ment. The classic odes that the student commits
to memory have been well weighed in their language,
every word bearing marks of nice discrimination.
The 'limæ labor' is concealed with artistic skill,
but it is observable by the student and enchains
his admiration. There is nothing of this kind in
the Bible. The narrative of David and Goliath,
or the feeding of the five thousand, or the miracle

referred to at the head of this chapter, are all told
in the simplest phraseology, intelligible alike to the
peasant or the child.

Nor are its contents marked with a design for
popularity. To call 'heaven and earth to witness
that they shall surely perish from off their good
land' is not the tone of one seeking to win personal
popularity with his hearers. Nor, in a later stage,
could the Voice proclaiming that 'Strait is the gate
and narrow is the way to life, and that few there be
that go in thereat,' be said to aim at alluring crowds.
The crowds did come, and hung by thousands round
His person, but, as if to show that such popularity
was not His aim, the Christ spoke reproachingly,
'Ye seek me because of the loaves and fishes which
ye got.' Often indeed the hearers were offended at
the teaching, and we are told that they walked with
Him no more. The Volume denounces the rich for
their worldliness, and tells the kings and potentates
of the earth that they are but men, and will be
judged by the same laws as their fellows. Language
like this was eminently calculated to rouse the
bitterest animosity in the wealthy and mighty,
whose influence or connivance the fawner seeks
with bended knee.

The Volume in its progress has been marked with

much *opposition*. Its readers have been denounced, imprisoned, put to death, simply for their tenacious adhesion to their sacred Volume. Its contents have in successive ages been mercilessly analysed, and the readers reproached with opprobrious hate. 'Ecrasez l'Infame' was the motto of Voltaire, and it is being imitated and acted upon to this day by not a few of Voltaire's countrymen. And yet in spite of persecution the most fiery, and criticism the most bitter, the Volume lives with a vitality increasingly tenacious, instead of becoming effete or exhausted with age; length of years seems but to increase its power of endurance.

And what are and have been its effects?

Its progress has been marked by nothing short of *revolution*. It has taught men the value of human life, previously counted as nothing. The Thracian mothers wept at the birth of a child into a world of trouble; the Spartan exposed for death the infant of delicate frame; even the most cultivated philosophers conceived the noblest termination to a life was the taking it away by one's own hand. The sacred Volume has combated these opinions, and combated them successfully. Wherever it has been received in its entirety, every human being becomes possessed of a new character in the eyes of his fellow-men ; to spare life, to alleviate pain, to lessen misery, become under its teaching high objects of human ambition. It speaks peace to the broken-hearted, and administers to the poor and suffering hopes and consolations unknown before. Hence, while not aiming at popularity, the Volume has been ever the friend of the masses of men, and has obtained a hold unknown by anything else since the world began. If it has failed to banish wars as yet, the number and the horrors have been gradually lessened. In pagan Rome and Greece, war was the normal condition, so that Livy describes it as something wonderful when a year transpires without a war. Contrast with this the desperate efforts now made to avert war by arbitration ; if it unhappily results, thousands of charitable hearts seek out the wounded and dying, and yearn for the comfort of the survivors. The almost extinction of duelling and of slavery are not the least trophies of the revolution the Volume has wrought.

Rising into the higher spheres of men, it has made kings and emperors bow before it, lay their hand on its pages, and swear to govern by its precepts. More astonishing still, the nations of the earth have agreed, in the main, to mark their years from the coming of Him who is made known to us in this Volume, and who yet seemed to have no beauty that men should desire Him.

Anyone contemplating this sketch of the Bible and its victorious march, might wonder with the same astonishment as the crowds round Peter and John and the restored cripple. The devout, and it may be added, the fair mind, will state that such a progress indicates that it is not man's work, but the work of God, and that the Bible is in reality what it is commonly called—the Word of God.

CHAPTER II.

THE BIBLE'S ACCOUNT OF ITSELF.

WHEN John the Baptist came preaching he was asked by his hearers—' What sayest thou of thyself? '

The same question may be asked of the Bible when its supporters claim for it that it is the Word of God. What account does the Bible give of itself? What origin does it claim ?

The answer to this will embrace three inquiries, which may be, however, pursued simultaneously :—

1. What account do the writers give of themselves ?

2. How were their writings regarded by the first receivers ?

3. How by their opponents ?

It is foreign to the subject of this treatise to inquire into the genuineness and authenticity of the books handed down to us. Those points must be proved and have been proved by other evidence. The books exist, and the acceptance of the Sacred Canon is taken for granted. Assuming this, our inquiry at present is limited to this point—Do they describe themselves as the work of man or of God ?

Taking the usual division of the books of Scripture into the Old and New Testament, the Old Testament shall be considered first.

It is impossible to open the pages of the Bible without observing how thoroughly the writers abstain from claiming any authority for themselves. They always represent themselves as the mouthpieces or agents of the Divine Being, they intimate in the plainest manner that their utterances are not their own.

This will appear from such passages as the following :—

When Moses was sent to visit his countrymen in Egypt, he hesitated to discharge his commission, owing, as he said, to his own poverty of speech. He was accordingly told to take Aaron his brother as a mouth-piece. On their first appearance before their countrymen (Exodus iv. 30, 31) we read :

'Aaron spake all the words which the Lord had spoken unto Moses, and did the signs in the sight of the people. And the people believed : and when they heard that the Lord had visited the children of Israel, . . . then they bowed their heads and worshipped.' Here is a case where the speakers' words would have had no acceptance *per se,* but the claim for them as the words of God procured a ready recognition.

There is a remarkable passage (Deut. xviii. 17–20) where Moses speaks of his own mission, the origin of his words, and the acceptance of that origin : ' The Lord said unto me, They have well spoken that which they have spoken. I will raise them up a prophet from among their brethren like unto thee, and will put my words in his mouth ; and he shall speak unto them all that I shall command him. And it shall come to pass that whosoever will not hearken unto my words which he shall speak in my name, I will require it of him.' It would be scarcely possible to find a passage more distinctly asserting a Divine origin, and the admission of it by hearer and speaker.

So again, in the case of *Joshua,* the successor of Moses (Joshua xxiv. 22), Joshua commences an address to his countrymen : ' Thus saith the Lord God of Israel—Ye are witnesses against yourselves that ye have chosen you the Lord, to serve Him.' And the people answered, ' We are witnesses.' Then it is added (ver. 26), ' and Joshua wrote these words in the book of the law of God.' These verses imply, (*a*) a Divine commission ; (*b*) the recognition of it ; (*c*) the perpetuation of it in a book.

Passing on to the subsequent books of the Old Testament, we have (2 Sam. xxiii. 1, 2) the royal psalmist using these words : ' The Spirit of the Lord spake by me, and His word was in my tongue,' indicating a clear perception by the speaker of an external power operating upon him, and that in consequence his words demand a hearing.

Isaiah (xxviii. 16), before uttering a solemn denunciation, prefaces it with the words, ' Wherefore hear the word of the Lord—thus saith the Lord.' So Jeremiah (ix. 15), ' Thus saith the Lord of Hosts, the God of Israel ; ' (xiii. 15) ' Hear ye, and give ear, . . . for the Lord hath spoken ; ' or again (vii. 1), ' The word that came to Jeremiah from the Lord,' a form with which he commences many of his utterances (xi. 1 ; xvi. 1), sometimes varied by the form ' These are the words that the Lord spake concerning Israel and concerning Judah.'

Ezekiel commences his prophecy (i. 1) with the words ' it came to pass as I was by the river Chebar, that the heavens were opened, and I saw visions of

God;' 'the word of the Lord came to Ezekiel the
priest;' he likewise abounds in the expressions,
'Thus saith the Lord God,' 'Moreover he said unto
me, Son of man.' This prophet abounds indeed in
marvellous instances of Divine influence over his
utterances, almost reducing himself to a passive instrument: thus (Ezek. iii. 14-16), 'So the Spirit
lifted me up and took me away, and I went in bitter-
ness . . . but the hand of the Lord was strong upon
me, and I came to them of the captivity, and I . . .
remained among them seven days. And at the end
of seven days, the word of the Lord came unto me,
saying, Son of man, hear the word at My mouth,
and give them warning from Me.'

Perhaps no more remarkable instance could be
found of a controlling and suggesting power over the
speaker, the instrument.

'The word of the Lord that came to Hosea ; ' 'the
burden of the word that came by Malachi ; ' 'in the
second year of Darius came the word of the Lord by
Haggai the prophet,' are the words with which each
commences his utterances, each humbly regarding
himself as the mouth-piece of a great Original.

We have thus to some extent seen what the
writers of the Old Testament say of themselves and
their utterances. It has also been stated concomi-

tantly that, on the occasion of their delivery, the
hearers have admitted their sacred origin.

Something more may be said on this point.

We are told (2 Chron. xxxiv.) that when King
Josiah commenced his reign, he was anxious for a
general restoration of the religious worship of his
country. His efforts need not be minutely described,
but during the progress Hilkiah the priest found a
copy of the Book of the Law of the Lord given by
Moses. This was taken to the king and read in his
presence. The effect on the young king was great :
we are told that the young king rent his clothes and
commanded the priest to inquire of the Lord, &c.
Now this passage, and the whole chapter of which it
is a portion, indicates how, in one of the worst times
of Jewish history, when the worship of God had died
out, it would be supposed that the Book of God, as it
had been forgotten, so it would be treated with con-
tempt. It was not so. So deeply engrained in the
Jewish mind was the sanctity attached to that Book
that even years of irreligion could not efface the
impression. This youth, the son of an impious king,
brought up amid the heathen abominations imported
by his father, had yet somehow received the national
belief as to that Word, that it was not to be received
as the word of man. His personal distress, along

with that of his colleague the priest, his proclamation of a national penitence and a national reformation, according to the tenour of the Book, his summoning the whole nation to hear read aloud the words of the Book (no words of flattery or pleasing import, but words of solemn denunciation and woe), the ready submission of his people to the youthful king's covenant, are indications of the national creed of which one article was, that the Book of the Law was the voice of God.

We may arrive at the same conclusion from another circumstance related in the life of Josiah's son. That son, Jehoiakim, had fallen off from the reforms instituted by his father, and the land was once more steeped in iniquity. Jeremiah instructed an amanuensis to take down from his mouth words which, he distinctly asserted, were spoken to him by God. These were read aloud before the assembled people. The impression was so great that a national fast was again proclaimed as a public humiliation. Intelligence of this and some subsequent proceedings was conveyed to the king himself. He ordered the roll to be read aloud in his hearing, and then he deliberately dissevered the leaves, and threw them in the fire before him. We are not concerned now with the childish folly of a king thus thinking,

by destroying the record, to defeat the purpose of
God. We are concerned only with this—that the
insane fury indicated that the words were regarded
as not mere human words. 'He believed and he
trembled.' But neither the solemn fast of the
people, nor the awe of the nobles, nor the fury of
the king would have taken place, if king, prophet,
and people had not recognised the old, old power
speaking to them with authority, as no man of
himself dare.

Hence we may sum up this part by saying that
a devout Israelite was impelled to acknowledge the
Old Testament as divine from the fact that from his
infancy he had seen it set apart from all other books,
by the universal consent and uniform practice of his
own nation. He saw the books treated with pious
reverence by the whole Hebrew people. He beheld
these books treasured up with devout care in the
synagogue, and brought forth Sabbath after Sabbath
from the sacred chest in those synagogues. He saw
those volumes unveiled and unrolled with holy veneration. He heard them proclaim messages to himself and his countrymen in burning words, but always
claiming credence for the message because it was
'Thus saith the Lord.' Before and after the reading
of those writings, he heard the accents of blessing and

praise addressed to God for the gift of those sacred writings.   He listened to their words recited with scrupulous care, and together with all his countrymen he venerated them with religious awe.[1]

To corroborate the above we may append the words of Josephus. 'We have not a multitude of books at variance with each other.   We have only twenty-two [according to the Jewish reckoning which counted the twelve minor prophets as one]; these contain the records of all time, and are the books which are rightly believed to be Divine.   We shew by our practice what our belief is as to these books. For although so long a time has elapsed since they were written, yet no one has ever ventured to make any additions to them, or to take anything from them, or to make any change in them.   And it is a principle innate in every Jew to regard these books as the Oracles of God, and to cleave to them, yea, and to die gladly for them.'

[1] The above reasoning is, in the main, Bishop Wordsworth's.

CHAPTER III.

CHRIST'S TREATMENT OF THE OLD TESTAMENT.

Treatment of Scripture by Christ—Did not seek to alter general
belief—His answers at temptation—Inference—Parable of
Lazarus—Scripture in synagogue—Answer to Sadducees—
Scribes—Before his trial—To disciples going to Emmaus.

ACCORDING to the usual account, the voice of prophecy was silent for about 400 years. Then came
the era of our Lord's ministry. This brings us to
consider in what light the Old Testament was regarded by our Blessed Lord Himself.

If the Jewish reverence for the Old Testament
was a superstition, we should expect that He Who
was the 'True Light that lighteth every man that
cometh into the world' would seek to rectify this
error, and censure His countrymen for ascribing the
Old Testament to God as its original. If the Old
Testament was merely the invention of men, or if
any portion of it had been false, the Christ would
never have made Himself an accomplice in passing
counterfeit coin, but would have reproved those who
attributed its origin to God.

Let us see His practice.

When He comes forth into public life after His baptism comes His temptation. In every case He answers the temptation by the words, ‘It is written.’ He on each occasion quotes from the books of Moses.

The Saviour thus lays down two principles :—

1. That the fact of a statement being found in Scripture is sufficient to command ready acceptance of its truth, and obedience to its precepts.

2. Also, as if by anticipation of the speculations of future times, that the books of Moses are to be received as part and parcel of Scripture, and as of equal force.

This second inference is strongly confirmed by the parable of the rich man and Lazarus. Our Saviour therein draws aside the veil that separates us from the unseen world, and shows to us Abraham in bliss and Lazarus admitted to his society. This spectacle is witnessed by the rich man, and amongst other requests he petitions the mission of Lazarus to his own brethren to effect their salvation. Abraham replies, ‘They have Moses and the prophets, let them hear them ;’ and he afterwards adds, ‘If they hear not Moses and the prophets, neither will they be persuaded though one rose from the dead.’

Jesus Christ here puts into the mouth of Abraham in heaven, as an immortal truth, that Moses and the prophets are the potent voice of God.

We read in the Gospels that it was His practice to go to the synagogues every Sabbath-day, to receive from the minister in charge the sacred rolls, to read a portion from them, and on that portion to base His own gracious words (would that they too had been recorded!). On one occasion He said, ' This day is this Scripture fulfilled,' and of the whole He maintained ' that it was easier for heaven and earth to pass away, than for one jot or one tittle of the Law to fail.' He thus stamped by His own sanction the belief of His countrymen as to the Word of God. But by such sanction He would be the reverse of ' The Truth' if He knew all the time that His countrymen were holding a groundless superstition.

Similar to the above is the occasion when He confronted the Sadducees who denied a resurrection, and who proposed to Him a case, as they supposed, incapable of solution. ' Ye do err,' He says, ' not knowing the Scriptures,' &c., and He immediately answers their supposed enigma from the only portion of Scripture which they received. It is remarkable that that portion of Scripture received by them is the portion in modern days most assailed. Yet from that single passage—the account of Moses at the burning bush, and from two words in that passage—the Saviour draws His refutation of their supposed difficulty. On another occasion the Christ Himself proposed a question to His cavillers. ' How say the Scribes' (Mark xii. 35, 36) 'that Christ is the Son of David? For David himself said by the Holy Ghost, The Lord said to my Lord,' &c. The important phrase here is—that the Saviour attributes David's message to the Holy Ghost.

When His trial was approaching, and a slight resistance was offered by His chosen few, the Saviour said, 'Thinkest thou that I could not pray . . . but how then would the Scriptures be fulfilled?' The inference being that the veracity of Scripture was paramount.

Finally, when He had overcome death and had risen again, we have recorded His encountering two of His disciples as they walked to Emmaus. They considered the recent events had prostrated their fondest hopes. His words are remarkable: 'Beginning at Moses and all the prophets, He expounded unto them in all the Scriptures the things concerning Himself.' He added, 'These are the words which I spake unto you, . . . that all things must be fulfilled which were written in the Law of

Moses, and in the prophets, and in the Psalms, concerning Me.' It would seem as if the Saviour's Divine mind had glanced down coming time, and had foreseen the assaults awaiting the faith, and the Volumes in which it is enshrined, the attacks on single portions and the disparagement of the whole. Hence the Saviour seems to have purposely given His impress to the common belief of His nation,—that all their books as received by them were rightly received, and were to continue to be received in their entirety, as the Scriptures of God.

CHAPTER IV.

TREATMENT OF THE OLD TESTAMENT BY THE APOSTLES.

Treatment of Scripture by apostles—Matthew sets forth Christ as fulfiller—Peter says same—Paul in Acts—Paul calls them 'oracles of God'—Peter and Paul state inspiration dogmatically.

It was only to be expected that the apostles and evangelists would follow in the Master's steps. As they have embodied His teaching in many other matters in a more dogmatic form, so have they treated the point of the origin of Scripture, and the light in which it is to be regarded.

St. Matthew abounds with such expressions as, 'All this was done that it might be fulfilled which was spoken by the prophets,' implying that an over-ruling Providence so ordered the course of events that His utterances by the mouth of His prophets should be proved true. On the first meeting of the apostolic college, Peter addresses the multitude of the disciples in these words:—'Men and brethren, this scripture must needs have been fulfilled, which the *Holy Ghost*, by the mouth of David, spake before concerning Judas.' In a subsequent chapter (Acts iii. 18) St. Peter concludes a long address to his countrymen with the words, 'But those things, which *God* before had shewn by the mouth of all His prophets, that Christ should suffer, He hath so fulfilled.'

In the next chapter we have the early Christian company assembled for prayer; in that prayer occur the words, 'Lord, Who by the mouth of Thy servant David hast said;' and again in the same prayer we have the words, 'Grant unto Thy servants that with all boldness they may speak Thy Word.'

In the last chapter of the Acts we have St. Paul addressing his countrymen (Acts xxviii. 25); when they agreed not among themselves he uses these words, 'Well spake the Holy Ghost by Esaias the prophet unto our fathers.'

In all these passages from the Acts there is the echo of the old belief, deeply embedded in every Jewish mind, as to the origin of their Scriptures. Two or three more instances, but still more marked, may suffice.

The third chapter of Romans commences with these words, 'What advantage then hath the Jew?'

'Much every way: chiefly, because that unto them were committed the oracles of God.' The striking passage here is 'the oracles of God,' and it is a point of exegesis, perhaps beyond the province of this essay, to elucidate all the depth of meaning implied by calling the Old Testament 'the oracles of God.' But the well-known importance attached to an oracle and oracular utterances indicates an equally high importance belonging to the utterances of Scripture, and that when Scriptures are called by St. Paul 'the oracles of *God*,' no more exalted description of them can well be conceived. The writer in that passage would further intimate that he could enumerate many other advantages as appertaining to the Jewish race, but, having stated that they are the custodians of the oracles of God, he stops short, as if, when he had claimed for them thus much, every other advantage was of minor consideration.[1]

St. Peter says (2 Peter i. 21), 'For the prophecy came not in old time by the will of man; but holy men of God spake as they were moved by the Holy Ghost.' And St. Paul, writing to Timothy (2 Tim. iii. 16), after calling to Timothy's mind the great blessings afforded him by his having from a

---

[1] The above reasoning is Professor Lee's.

child been trained in the Scriptures, states dogmatically that 'All Scripture is given by inspiration of God.'

On this conviction St. Paul writes through the whole of the Epistle to the Hebrews (assuming that epistle to be Paul's or Pauline), for his whole argument is to point out to his countrymen the intention of the Holy Ghost in the elaborate details of their gorgeous liturgy.

All that has been said hitherto has reference to the Old Testament, and the inquiry has been purposely limited thereto; for the assailants of the doctrine before us especially level their shafts against the early portion of the Sacred Volume.

Of a truth both Testaments are indissolubly united; they cannot be dissevered. The whole of the early portion was designed for, and had its completion in, the latter. Whoever would impugn the former must, from what has been shown, make the Saviour of mankind a liar, and must fling in His teeth His own charge against the Pharisees of being 'a blind leader of the blind.' Such a man must set up his unsupported conception against the established belief of a whole nation for thousands of years, the original recipients of the documents so impugned.

CHAPTER V.

ORIGIN OF THE NEW TESTAMENT.

New Testament—St. John says why he wrote—New Testament does not state origin directly—Not infer from Acts that St. Paul wrote anything—Christ's charge and promise to apostles—Their mission described—Aid promised of complete inspiration in speech—Same to be expected in their writings—Paul claims it when writing Epistles—Says he received Gospel by revelation—Peter about Paul's Epistles.

WE have now to pass on to the New Testament, and consider whether it is counted as speaking words more than those of men.

That it was designed like the Old Testament as a memorial for after times St. John has not obscurely intimated, when he announced the motive that led to the composition of his Gospel. 'These are written that ye might believe that Jesus is the Christ, the Son of God, and that believing, ye might have life through His name.' Of this destination of the Sacred Writings for every future age, a striking proof is afforded by the fact that, while combating the errors and heresies of their day, the apostles never descend into details, neither naming the leaders of the heresies, nor describing the factions with which they had to contend. There is an exception to this in St. Paul's letters to Timothy, where he speaks of Hymeneus and Alexander (1 Tim. i. 20), and Hymeneus and Philetus (2 Tim. ii. 17, 18). But these seem to be remarks of a personal character, addressed to Timothy as a minister of the Church of Christ; they do not come in a general epistle. And yet it must be admitted that the New Testament affords no *direct* information as to its origin, and that it is silent as to the collection of its several parts. The sacred writers seem to take no notice of matters respecting which we might have anticipated information would be given. Thus the Acts, which enter with minuteness into St. Paul's history, give not the slightest hint that he ever wrote an epistle. But there are arguments founded upon external testimony and internal presumption.

Before our Blessed Lord left this world, He charged His apostles (Matt. xxviii. 19, 20), 'Go ye therefore, and teach all nations. . . . Teaching them to observe all things whatsoever I have commanded you : and, lo! I am with you alway, even unto the end of the world.'

And again (Acts i. 8), 'But ye shall receive power, after that the Holy Ghost is come upon you :

and ye shall be witnesses unto Me both in Jerusalem, and in all Judæa, and in Samaria, and unto the uttermost part of the earth.'

To which may be added (John xx. 21), ' Peace be unto you; as My Father hath sent Me, even so send I you.'

In consequence of this commission the apostles went forth to make disciples of all nations, and to promulgate to them the doctrines, the ordinances, and the mysteries of the kingdom of God. They were to bear the keys of the kingdom of heaven, so that whatsoever they should bind or loose upon earth should be bound or loosed in heaven. He had breathed on them, saying, ' Receive ye the Holy Ghost,' and, so fortified, they could reveal the wondrous character of the Word made flesh, and of the Creator so abased as to take upon Him the form of a creature and to die upon the cross. They reported His inimitable words, and acted as His ambassadors, as if Christ spake by them (2 Cor. v. 20).

For the performance of this work they had special promises given them, not only on His final departure but on other previous occasions; as if to assimilate their mission to that of the prophets of old, who always commenced their announcements with the words, ' Thus saith the Lord.'

Such promises were these :—'When they deliver you up, take no thought how or what ye shall speak ; for it shall be given you in that same hour what ye shall speak. For it is not ye that speak, but the Spirit of your Father which speaketh in you ' (Matt. x. 19, 20).

Again, we have a similar promise (Luke xii. 11, 12): 'When they bring you unto the synagogues, and unto magistrates, and powers, take ye no thought how or what thing ye shall answer, or what ye shall say : for the Holy Ghost shall teach you in the same hour what ye ought to say.'

So again (Mark xiii. 11): 'But when they shall . . . deliver you up, take no thought beforehand what ye shall speak, neither do ye premeditate ; but whatsoever shall be given you in that hour, that speak ye : for it is not ye that speak, but the Holy Ghost.'

On these different occasions the Lord assured His apostles that the most complete inspiration should regulate their language in the most difficult and important moments of their ministry.

It is evident, therefore, that if the most entire guidance were assured to them for the dangers of each coming day, to fortify them for all assaults before tribunals, whether of priests, governors, or kings; if they were certified that the very words of their answers should be supplied to them by the operation of the Holy Ghost, it is evident that the same guidance would be vouchsafed to them when they put their words in writing, and continued ' the oracles of God.' For in so doing their words would not be for a passing day, but for all succeeding ages; and it would be the height of absurdity to suppose that the Spirit of God should supply them, without any premeditation on their part, with words to address a Festus or an Agrippa, and yet that the suggesting guidance should be withdrawn when they proceeded to express indelibly words for *all* time, embodying the everlasting Gospel.[1]

We are not without intimation that the apostles themselves considered that, when writing, the same inspiration was guaranteed.

Take, for instance, St. Paul's own convictions as to the origin of his own utterances (Ephes. iii. 3, 4 5): ' As I *wrote* afore in few words; whereby, when ye read, ye may understand my knowledge in the mystery of Christ, which in other ages was not made known unto the sons of men, as it is now revealed unto His holy *apostles* and prophets by the Spirit.'

---

[1] The above reasoning is Gaussen's.

D

In this passage St. Paul distinctly asserts that he wrote under the guidance of the Holy Spirit, and that his utterance as an *apostle* is to be placed on a level with that of a prophet.

Again (Romans xvi. 25, 26), St. Paul writes, 'Now to Him that is of power to stablish you according to my gospel, and the preaching of Jesus Christ (according to the revelation of the mystery, which was kept secret since the world began, but now is made manifest, and by the *scriptures of the prophets*, according to the commandment of the ever-lasting God, made known to all nations for the obe-dience of faith), &c. In this passage it is to be observed that St. Paul calls the writings which make known the faith 'the scriptures of the prophets,' claiming for them the same acceptance, as being under the same guidance as the prophets of old, who spake as they were moved by the Holy Ghost.

The same inference might be drawn from the very words with which St. Paul begins his epistles.

'Paul, a servant of Jesus Christ, called to be an apostle,' are the words with which he begins the first epistle in the canonical arrangement. 'Paul, an apostle, not of men, neither by man, but by Jesus Christ,' are the first words of the Epistle to the Galatians. 'Paul, an apostle of Jesus Christ by the

will of God,' are the first words of the Epistle to the
Ephesians.   He glories in the name of 'apostle,'
he considers that office as having the highest of
pentecostal gifts (1 Cor. xii. 28), and that with the
aid of such gifts he writes his epistles.

There is a very remarkable expression in one of
the Epistles of St. Peter (2 Peter iii. 15).   It was
written some twenty or thirty years after the
pentecostal effusion, and from it we should infer that
many, if not all, of the books of the New Testament
were already in existence.   The words are these:
' Our beloved brother Paul also, according to the
wisdom given unto him, hath written unto you ; as
also in *all his epistles*, speaking in them of these
things, in which are some things . . . which they
. . . wrest: as they do also the other Scriptures, unto
their own destruction.'   From this passage the inference is, that the epistles of St. Paul were already in
circulation, had been read aloud in the churches,
and St. Peter classes them on a level with the other
Scriptures, having the same primal Originator, and
entitled to the same acceptance by the Church of
God.

CHAPTER VI.

MODUS OPERANDI OF INSPIRATION.

How would inspiration be imparted—(1) *Visions*, such as to Moses, Daniel, Ezekiel, Paul—(2) *Voices*: when Moses received the Law; Samuel—(3) *Dreams*: Jacob's ladder, Joseph with Holy Child, Peter on housetop—(4) *Intuitions*.

THIS Divine influence, commonly called inspiration, when applied to any portion of the Holy Scriptures is said in Scripture to make it θεόπνευστος (2 Tim. iii. 16), the word θεοπνευστία, indicating the practice, does not, the writer believes, occur in Scripture. Several inquiries at once present themselves.

1. By what media would the writer or speaker receive his inspiration?

2. What phenomena may be observed as attaching to that influence?

3. To what extent would this inspiration influence the recipients?

4. Some reference may be made to the objections which have been or may be urged against the acceptance of Scripture as inspired.

1. We have first to consider the *media* by which inspiration would influence its recipients.

One of the most frequent methods referred to in Scripture is by means of *visions.*

Visions would include any communications conveyed through an object of *sight.* Such would be the instruction given to Moses at the burning bush to go forth as the deliverer of his countrymen. Such again would be that in Exod. xiii. 21, 22, ' The Lord went before them by day in a pillar of a cloud, to lead them the way ; and by night in a pillar of fire, to give them light.' [1]

Another such would be that seen by *Daniel* and those around him (v. 5): ' In the same hour came forth fingers of a man's hand, and wrote . . . . upon the plaster of the wall.'

Or again, those recorded by *Ezekiel*, one specimen being (viii. 3), ' And he put forth the form of a hand, ... and the Spirit lifted me up between the earth and the heaven, and brought me in the visions of God to Jerusalem,' &c.

Such also might be called the appearance of our Lord to *St. Paul.* It has been doubted whether St. Paul actually saw the Lord Jesus when on his

---

[1] The 'media' here described are suggested by the work of Bishop Hinds.

way to Damascus, but he speaks himself of personal appearances, and makes them the ground of his apostleship. 'Am I not an apostle? Have I not seen Jesus Christ our Lord?' (1 Cor. ix. 1); and he distinctly asserts that he received the Gospel which he preached not from any human being, but by revelation from Jesus Christ Himself (Galat. i. 12).

2. Another mode of communication was by *voices*, and would apply to all revelations communicated by the sense of *hearing*. These would probably be the most frequent manifestations of spiritual guidance. The recipient saw nothing, but heard a voice unmistakable and authoritative. Such would be the voice giving *Moses* the Law from Mount Sinai, and those frequent occasions in the Pentateuch when we have his expression, 'The Lord said unto me!' Such would be the manifestations to *Samuel* when a child. It is called indeed in Scripture a 'vision,' but there does not appear from the context to have been anything actually seen, and thus it will be differenced off from those referred to above under the head of visions.

3. A third form of direction was by *dreams*. This form of manifestation, if by night, seems to have been called ὄναρ; if by day, ἔκστασις. Of the former kind would be the representation to Jacob in

his dream, the instruction to Joseph to depart with the Holy Child into Egypt, and, again, to return on the death of Herod.

Of the latter kind would be the manifestation to Peter when he went on the housetop (Acts x. 10).

4. Another form would be by instinctive impulses, now commonly called *intuitions*. This form does not appear to have been an address either to the senses or the imagination, but to have operated on the inclinations. There was no perceptible medium, but the instrument felt the power, and according to its energising influence, prophets and apostles spake as they were moved by the Holy Ghost.

CHAPTER VII.

PHENOMENA SHOWN BY THE Θεόπνευστος.

Phenomena accompanying the above—(1) Influence for a particular purpose, *e.g.* Elisha, Ahijah, Balaam, man of God to
Jeroboam, &c., Paul to go to Jerusalem—(2) Recipient was conscious—(3) Writers knew origin of utterances—(4) Often not
conscious of full meaning: passage of Peter; Ezekiel's case—
(5) Did not exempt from personal error: Nathan's mistake;
Saul; Peter at Antioch; Agabus.

THERE were certain *phenomena* which were concomi-
tant with, or characteristic of, these Divine influences,
as described in Scripture, and which require separate
notice.

1. The influence seems to have been for a *particular purpose*, and seldom if ever *continuous*,
though this latter feature has been contested, and
the reverse stoutly maintained.

An instance of this would be the case of the
prophet *Elisha*. He seems, according to the sacred
narrative, to have been as powerfully influenced by
the Spirit of God as any prophet in Scripture. And
yet on one occasion we read (2 Kings iv. 27), in

reference to the Shunammite, 'And when she came to the man of God to the hill, she caught him by the feet: but Gehazi came near to thrust her away. And the man of God said, Let her alone; for her soul is vexed within her: and the Lord hath hid it from me, and *hath not told me.*'

This is at once an admission by the prophet that his power was limited, and that the prophetic gift was not with him at all times.

In contrast with this would be the case stated (1 Kings xiv. 4, 5): 'Jeroboam's wife . . . arose, and went to Shiloh, and came to the house of Ahijah : but Ahijah could not see. . . . And the Lord said unto Ahijah, Behold, the wife of Jeroboam cometh to ask a thing of thee for her son; for he is sick: thus and thus shalt thou say unto her; for it shall be,' &c. Here we have a piece of information revealed for a specific purpose to a prophet of whom scarcely any other utterances are known, when the information for a parallel case was denied to Elisha; as if to keep constantly impressed on the recipient's mind that he was but an instrument. Similar to the above might be the case of *Balaam*, of whose life we have but one episode; and yet he is on that one occasion made the mouth-piece of a prophecy that lived in the memory of the children of Israel for 1,500 years

(Numb. xxiv. 17). Such also might be the cases of
the *man of God* sent to Jeroboam as he stood by
the altar to burn incense, and who gives a distinct
utterance (and the only one recorded of him) prophetic of Josiah ; also the old prophet that dwelt in
Bethel, who became the mouth-piece of a denunciation against the above peccant man of God (1 Kings
xiii. 2-21). Such may be considered also the case of
St. Paul when (Acts xx. 22, 23) he states, ' I go
bound in the spirit unto Jerusalem, not knowing the
things that shall befall me there, save that the Holy
Ghost witnesseth in every city, saying that bonds
and afflictions abide me.' As if the Holy Ghost
guided him into all truth as to the subjects of his
great mission, but did not reveal details of his
personal life.

2. A further particular to be noticed is, that the
recipients were in each case in a state of *consciousness*. Jacob when he beheld the ladder, the child
Samuel, Joseph when ' warned in a dream,' Peter
when in a trance, were thoroughly conscious of all
that took place though the bodily action was sus-
pended. The impression was permanent, and so
felt by the recipient that he acted as if a bodily
presence had been before him. This will difference off all Biblical writers from the μάντεις

and προφῆται of heathen divination. The only exception to the above remark might be 1 Sam. xix. 24.

3. The writers knew the *origin* of their utterances. 'Thus saith the Lord' is their habitual prefix; 'only the word which the Lord giveth me, that will I speak,' is the language of the basest of them (Balaam). Even though the record of his utterance might be contemptuously destroyed, yet the writer at the peril of his life (as Jeremiah) repeated his mission, for he knew it was of God.

4. Yet, though cognisant of the *origin*, the speakers were often not cognisant of the *full* meaning of their utterances. There is a very remarkable passage in St. Peter clearly stating this (1 Peter i. 10, 11): 'Of which salvation the prophets have enquired and searched diligently, who prophesied of the grace that should come unto you: searching what, or what manner of time, the Spirit of Christ which was in them did signify, when it testified beforehand the sufferings of Christ, and the glory that should follow.' As if the speakers delivered their utterance by an irresistible impulse, and then exerted thereon their mental faculties to fathom the tendency and meaning.

This would be the case with such utterances as

those of Ezekiel, when, after delivering his commission (Ezek. xx.), he closes it with the words, 'Ah
Lord God! they say of me, Doth he not speak
parables?' Or, that marvellous case when he was
ordered to speak to the people in the morning, and
in the evening his wife should die, and yet he was
forbidden to shed a tear of lamentation. Such a
dealing, while it showed to him and all around that
his mission was from God, yet in the process might
well appear mysterious, baffling human comprehen-
sion.

5. The inspiring influence did not exempt them
from *personal error as men*, except when so
influenced.

A few instances may be mentioned :—

a. When David first conceived the idea of build-
ing a temple to the Lord, he mentioned the project
to Nathan the prophet, who replied, 'Go, do all that
is in thine heart, for the Lord is with thee.' Nathan
there spoke simply as an ordinary man ; the project
seemed a noble one and worthy of commendation.
After this we read that the word of the Lord came to
Nathan instructing him to recall his words, adding
that the house proposed should be built by David's
son and not by David himself (2 Sam. vii. 2-13).

b. In the history of Saul, after his anointing by

Samuel, we are told that Samuel promised him the gift of the Spirit of God (1 Sam. x. 6), and that so it took place; yet very soon after occurred the judgment on Saul for the matter of Agag (1 Sam. xv.), and then we are told that the Spirit of the Lord departed from Saul.

c. So when Samuel was sent to anoint David, his personal inclination would have been to anoint the elder brother (1 Sam. xvi. 6), but a Divine intimation prompted him to do otherwise.

d. Peter had been breathed upon by our Lord, and received the Holy Ghost; he had also received the pentecostal gifts. Yet in personal conduct he was a man, and Paul distinctly states that he withstood Peter to the face, because he was to be blamed (Galat. ii. 11).

e. Agabus (Acts xxi. 11) distinctly states that he is speaking by the Holy Ghost when he tells of the troubles awaiting St. Paul, and would seem to be using his Divine knowledge to defeat the Divine purposes.

The cases of Balaam and the old prophet of Bethel have been already referred to as instances of the prophetic gift existing in men of immoral character, and impelling them even against their own inclinations.

CHAPTER VIII.

THEORIES AS TO THE EXTENT OF THE INSPIRING INFLUENCE ON THE RECIPIENT.

To what extent did inspiration affect recipients—Various theories:
1. Coleridge; 2. Morell; 3. Macnaught; 4. Westcott, and
Harold Browne; 5. Ebrard; 6. Bishop Wilson; 7. Schleiermacher; 8. Hinds; 9. Tomline; 10. Lee; 11. Gaussen;
12. Manning; 13. Wilson, of Clifton ; 14. Pollock.

AFTER observing the above phenomena, a natural
inquiry will be—to *what extent* shall it be said that
θεοπνευστία influences the writers of Scripture. In
answer to this have arisen the various theories or
definitions which have obtained weight.

It would be an act of presumption to attempt to
sit in judgment, and pronounce authoritatively as to
which is to be accepted, to the exclusion of all others.
It would seem sufficient for the purposes of this
essay to state the various theories or definitions,
with such observations upon them as may seem
pertinent to their due consideration.

1. Whatever finds me bears witness that it has

proceeded from a Holy Spirit: in the Bible there is more that finds me than I have experienced in all other books put together; but I protest against the doctrine which requires me to believe that not only what finds me, but all that exists in the Sacred Volume, was not only composed by men under the actuating influence of the Holy Spirit, but was likewise dictated by an Infallible Intelligence, and that they were each and all divinely inspired.— COLERIDGE.

2. Inspiration, as applied to the Holy Scriptures, does not include either miraculous powers, verbal dictation, or any distinct commission from God. It consists in the impartation of clear intuitions of moral and religious truth to the mind by extra-ordinary means, a potency which every man to a certain degree possesses.—MORELL.

3. Inspiration is that action of the Divine Spirit by which, apart from any idea of infallibility, all that is good in man, beast, or matter is originated and sustained.—MACNAUGHT.

4. Westcott ('Introduction of Study of Gospel') gives no definition, nor does he lay down any distinct theory, but makes some statements, thus—

'Inspiration is the correlative of Revelation; both operations imply a supernatural extension of the field of man's spiritual vision. By inspiration we conceive that man's natural powers are quickened, so that man contemplates the truth with a Divine intuition. By revelation the dark veil is removed from the face of things. Inspiration is the direct intelligible communication of the Divine Will to chosen messengers; it is bestowed for some special end to which it is exactly proportioned; it is *dynamical*, the human powers of the Divine messenger act according to their natural laws, even when those powers are supernaturally strengthened. Man is not converted into a mere machine; the purely organic theory rests on no Scripture authority, and is at variance with the whole form and fashion of the Bible.'

The remarks of Bishop Harold Browne,[1] if the writer understands them rightly, are nearly to the same purport.

5. The Bible *contains* the Word of God; there exist imperfections in Scripture resulting from limited knowledge, or inadvertence, or defective memory in its authors, though these imperfections are often restricted to unimportant matters.—EBRARD.

---

[1] *Aids to Faith*, edited by Archbishop Thomson.

6. There are degrees of inspiration: inspiration of *suggestion*, the Spirit dictating minutely every part; of *direction*, when it only directs the mind in the exercise of its powers; of *elevation*, lifting it up to comprehend truth otherwise unattainable; of *superintendency*, checking and controlling the statement made.—Bishop DANIEL WILSON.

7. Inspiration consists in aiding the awakenment and elevation of our religious consciousness, in presenting to us a mirror of the history of Christ, and in giving us the letter through which the spirit of truth may be brought home to the human heart.—SCHLEIERMACHER.

8. Inspiration is the being miraculously enabled either to receive a Divine revelation or to execute a Divine commission.—Bishop HINDS.

9. That controlling influence over the writers of Scripture which guaranteed exemption from doctrinal error.—Bishop TOMLINE.

10. Inspiration is that Divine influence under which *all* the parts of the Bible have been committed to writing, whether they contain an account of extraordinary historical facts, or the narrative of supernatural revelation.—Professor LEE.

E

11. Inspiration is the term used for the mysterious power which the Divine Spirit put forth on the authors of the Scripture of the Old and New Testament, in order to their composing them as they have been received by the Church of God at their hands. This miraculous operation of the Holy Ghost had not the *writers* themselves for its object—these were only His instruments, and were soon to pass away ; its objects were the *Holy books* themselves.— Professor GAUSSEN.

12. Scripture has God for its author, and is inspired not only in faith and morals, but in all its parts which bear on faith, including matters of fact. The books are inspired because the writers were inspired to write them. They are not inspired *books* unless they come from inspired *men.*—Cardinal MANNING.

13. Inspiration is an illumination in all that concerns religious truth, and the only imaginable revelation is gradual, historical, and accommodated. —Mr. WILSON, of Clifton.

14. We must hold that the genuine Scriptures are all from God Himself, infallibly sure and true. If it be otherwise, they would be the infinite source of perplexity and confusion, not of truth and unity. —Archdeacon POLLOCK.

CHAPTER IX.

EXAMINATION OF THE ABOVE THEORIES.

Examination of above—Gaussen's closely—Somewhat supported
by Christ's use of one word—If parts rejected, where to end ?

SOME diffidence may be naturally felt in attempting to criticise the previous theories, propounded as
many of them are by men of established fame. It
is hoped that the following remarks thereon may be
legitimate :—

Coleridge's theory (No. 1) if worked out would
either make each man a Bible to himself, or would
reduce the Bible to a mere ordinary book, not speaking with authority, a mere human compilation, to
be accepted or rejected without incurring any responsibility either way.

2. Morell's is a denial of any miraculous element.
If accepted, then the writers who tell us positively
that they 'heard a voice saying' or saw a hand, &c.,
must be taxed as fabricators of falsehood.

3. The third (Macnaught's) is open to numbers
of objections—perhaps the most fatal is that the
Bible ceases to be a guide ; each man is himself the

decider of what is good.   He does not *learn* from
his Bible, but the reverse.

4. Westcott's views are very obscure, if that
description may be pardoned.   They seem to be
open to two objections.   If inspiration be considered
simply *dynamical*—*i.e.* an expansion of a man's
natural powers—it would be expected that the same
man would be at all times and for all purposes inspired.   And yet they distinctly state at times ' the
Lord hath hid it from me.'

Westcott also flatly denies that the speaker or
writer is ever a mere machine.   Instances have been
mentioned above which, if true in fact, reduce the
speaker to a mere instrument, such, for instance, as
the revelations of Ezekiel.   With such cases Westcott's theory seems not to be reconcilable.

Theories 5 and 7.   Those of Ebrard and Schleiermacher would make inspiration dependent on a man's
purity of heart ; if one man has a purer heart than
another he must be more inspired.   So that if a
man of the present generation were to be found of
higher religious tone and more consistent life than
an apostle—say St. Peter—he would have a higher
intuition of Divine things, and know Christian truth
more infallibly.

Mr. Wilson's theory (No. 13) seems to have been

devised from the unwillingness to admit any miraculous element in religion.   That is the fashionable scepticism of the day, and the definition or explanation seems ' accommodated ' thereto.   But such accommodation would appear to be contrary to fact. ' God who at sundry times, and in divers manners, spake in times past to the fathers by the prophets, hath in these latter days spoken to us by His Son.' That Son promised to His apostles that the Holy Ghost should put into their mouths what to speak, and, by inference, what to write.   But one of the apostles distinctly states that prophecy (as understood in Scripture) should cease.   That Son also promised to His apostles that He would be with them always, even to the end of the world.   But surely that comforting assurance has no reference to inspiration such as we have been considering, and will not justify the assertion made by this theorist that it is ' continuous.'   If so, the most extravagant claims as to absolution, indulgences, the incorporation of new dogmas—as the immaculate conception—must be accepted as being valid developments of inspiration.

Of all the above theories, two stand out as pre-eminently deserving attention :—

1. That inspiration is plenary and verbal.

2. That it guarantees freedom from doctrinal error.

CHAPTER X.

EXAMINATION OF THEORIES (*continued*).

Objections to Gaussen—Text undecided—Books disputed—
Passages stating not facts—Writers reduced to machines—
Church of England gives no definition—Falls back on Scripture—Three passages quoted—Inference—Tomline's definition a safe one.

THE most potent exponent of plenary and verbal
inspiration is Professor Gaussen. Though this
theory is most vehemently attacked at the present
day, there is more to be said in its favour than may
at first sight appear. One instance may be given.
For observe how our Saviour will build a whole
argument on a *single word*.

On a memorable occasion the Jews took up
stones to stone Him. He remonstrated, and they
answered, 'For a good work we stone Thee not, but
for blasphemy, and because that Thou, being a man,
makest thyself God.' His reply is this: 'Is it not
written in your *law*, I said, Ye are gods? If he
called them gods, to whom the Word of God came,
and the Scripture cannot be broken; say ye of Him,
whom the Father hath sanctified, and sent into the

world, Thou blasphemest; because I said, I am the Son of God?' It is with the former part of this passage that we are concerned.

a. Christ, being charged with blasphemy, rested for His defence on a simple appeal to the Scriptures, and to their letter. It was open to Him to have met the charge by other arguments, but He simply answered, 'It is written,' as in the case previously alluded to of His temptation, and of course such an appeal was utterly worthless if whatsoever was written was not the very Word of God.

b. It is to be observed further that the Saviour did not say, 'Is it not written in the Psalms?' from which the quotation is taken (Ps. lxxxii.), but, 'Is it not written in your *Law?*' Their Scriptures were commonly included under the title of the Law, the Prophets, and the Psalms, and our Saviour, by using the expression, 'Is it not written in your *Law?*' appears to maintain that the whole volume of Scripture was equally at His service, and that He could cite any portion of it as of supreme and infallible authority.

This appeal would have been valueless, it would have been dishonest, if any portion, if a single word, was open to exception.

c. Be it observed further that Christ builds His

argument, not on the passage, but on a *single word*, the word 'gods.' The force of His argument lies in the use of that word by the Psalmist. In the first verse of that Psalm David says, 'God standeth in the congregation of the mighty; He judgeth among the gods,' and now he repeats, '*I* have said, Ye are gods, ... but ye shall,' &c. David makes it a personal remark, and our Saviour's cavillers might have said that David was not an inspired prophet, he wrought no miracle to establish such a claim, and whenever he personally wished to know the will of God, it was revealed to him through the agency of a prophet or seer. This passage, spoken as it was in bitter irony, *might* have been cavilled at as of no inspired weight on that account, and yet it was *not* objected to by the Christ's bitterest opponents.

d. The phrase moreover is in the highest degree figurative. It is thought to have been an expression borrowed from the heathen. The Psalm itself is a poem, called forth by some act of magisterial oppression, and the Psalmist is rebuking their tyranny.

Putting all these points together—that the passage in question was not a prominent one in the writings of the Psalmist, that the Psalmist's writings gain the character of inspiration by being included in the Law, that the passage is poetical, and the single word relied on is figurative in character, and might be counted as David's own rather than a suggested one—yet we see that on that little word in that little poem Christ was prepared to base His whole mission from His Father. His opponents called Him a blasphemer, and He *was* one in reality if that word cited in His defence did not justify His claim ; but it *was* cited because it was in the ' Scripture that cannot be broken.'

It has been objected to this, and to other references to our Saviour's quotations and inferences, that He spake as and with the prejudices of a Jewish Rabbi, and that He ' accommodated ' Himself to His hearers. Both these statements may be flatly denied. He never claimed to speak, nor was recognised as speaking, as a Jewish Rabbi, and He never ' accommodated ' Himself to His hearers. His whole life and teaching were a protest against the system of ' accommodation ' practised by the professed instructors of His day. Had He stooped to it perhaps He had not died.[1]

So that on the whole we may state that, with such an instance before us of our Saviour's use of one word, the argument for the Verbal Inspiration

The above reasoning is, in the main, Archdeacon Pollock's.

of Scripture is very strong, and its opponents incur a very grave responsibility.

The theory gathers weight from the natural inquiry of its supporters : If we once commence striking out words and passages from the received Scriptures, for whatever reasons, doubtless satisfactory to the objectors, where will it end ? Under the process of excision the Old Testament, and much of the New Testament, will vanish as did early Roman history under the axe of Niebuhr. The pious mind will have no guide of authority, the grieving heart nothing whereon to lean, for the very props which may have been the comfort and stay of thousands will be ruthlessly torn away.

Against this view of the extent of inspiration objections can be easily raised.

1. (*a*) That the very words whose plenary inspiration is so stoutly insisted on are often of doubtful validity. (*b*) The text of some parts is admittedly corrupt ; whole passages are thought to be spurious, as in the Epistles of St. John. (*c*) Whole books have been the subject of debate as to their admissibility or retention in the Sacred Canon. (*d*) And it is still, and perhaps ever will be, an open question whether St. Matthew ever wrote in Greek— *i.e.* whether the Gospel, of which the advocates of

this theory maintain every word to be inspired, is actually a gospel at all. How, then, shall we insist on Verbal Inspiration as to words, whose existence, as it were, hangs in the balance ?

2. The defender of this theory is often put to considerable difficulty in dealing with such passages as 'The sun knoweth his going down,' 'He hath made the round world so fast,' &c., and numbers of others. These come under the cognisance of the . expositor, who can, in many cases, account for them satisfactorily under other aspects of inspiration than the theory before us.

3. It is also objected that the writers of Scripture according to this theory are reduced to mere machines, an objection strongly dwelt upon by writers entitled to great respect ; yet this objection may not be considered so weighty if it be remembered how frequently the recipient of inspiration, though conscious, was at times certainly a mere instrument. What else was Ezekiel when he said, ' I spake to the people in the morning, and at evening my wife died.' He was a sign to his countrymen, but he delivered a message mechanically, of which he himself knew not the full import.

It is to be observed that the Church of England nowhere lays down any definition or dogmatic statement of inspiration. In the sixth Article she asserts that 'Holy Scripture containeth all things necessary to salvation: so that whatsoever is not read therein, nor may be proved thereby, is not to be required of any man, that it should be believed as an article of the Faith, or be thought requisite or necessary to salvation.' She also rehearses the Nicene Creed, which asserts that the Holy Ghost spake by the prophets. But the Church nowhere lays down to what extent the Holy Ghost spake by the prophets, using the word prophet in its wider meaning. The Church seems thus to throw us back on Scripture: 'that holy men of God spake as they were moved by the Holy Ghost;' and again, 'From a child thou hast been taught to know the Scriptures, which are able to make thee wise unto salvation;' also, 'All Scripture is given by inspiration of God, and is profitable for doctrine, for reproof, for correction, for instruction in righteousness.'

These three passages, whilst they assert the highest claim for the authority of Scripture, seem to point out the grand purposes which should be the primary at least, if not the sole, objects of our consideration in perusing its pages: that it is able to make us wise unto salvation, and that it is profitable for doctrine and guidance of life. It is from disregard of this prime object that many have criticised its pages as if it professed to be a guide to astronomy, geology, and physical science generally. These are left for man's own development, just as he has developed the architecture with which he raises his buildings, or the clothing that covers his person Putting all together, most thoughtful and moderate minds will accept the view of inspiration laid down by Bishop Tomline, that, 'Inspiration is that guiding and controlling operation of the Holy Ghost, by which the writings of Scripture are guaranteed from doctrinal error.' Some of the other theories quoted above centre round this, even Cardinal Manning's. For that writer in explaining his view as to what in Scripture is binding on the faith of a Catholic, whilst he refers to the councils of his Church as ultimate authority, is careful to append the saving clause '*de fide et moribus*.' Such a description in no way detracts from the dignity of Scripture, it does not attempt to limit or define what Scripture, and the Church under its guidance, have not defined, and it avoids the great danger of attempting to prove too much.

CHAPTER XI.

SOME OBJECTIONS.

Peculiar difficulties—Office of expositor—Two stated.

IT is not within the scope of this essay to refute or explain the various cavils raised against *portions* of Scripture.   Such are—the Mosaic cosmogony, the difficulties about the Deluge, the story of Joshua commanding the sun to stand still, the conduct of Deborah commending assassination, and others. Nor is it our province to state whether Paul spoke as a man or by inspiration when he requested his cloke and parchments to be brought, or such a passage as 1 Cor. vii. 25, where he appears (but in fact only appears) to speak doubtfully as to the advice he tenders. All these are matters of exegesis, and come rather under the cognisance of the expositor of Scripture.   In many cases they have received satisfactory answers?   Take, for instance, the case of Deborah.

It has been said, Here is a prophetess leading the armies of the people of God against their foes, and

when she is told that the commander of the opposing
army has been assassinated under circumstances from
which human nature recoils, this inspired prophetess
exults in the deed and holds it up for admiration.
This transaction has been severely commented on and
deservedly so, but it has been cited as an instance
against 'all Scripture' being 'given by inspiration of
God.' That is an unfair view of the case. Deborah
was a prophetess inspired for a particular purpose—
to rouse her countrymen to manly patriotism against
their grinding oppressor. She was not a writer of
Scripture, and is no more to be held up for imitation
than Samson subsequently. Who would hold up
Samson as a model? and yet the Spirit of God was
upon him for a particular purpose. Deborah's conduct is recorded, and it is abundantly instructive for
correction. It indicates the moral degradation to
which a community may sink, that, as with the
people so with the priests, the moral vision will become distorted, and the primary feelings of humanity
extinguished. The passage is rightly written for our
learning, for our correction, but not for imitation.

(Bishop Wordsworth and others give different
explanations from the above.)

Nothing has been said about the modes by which
Scripture has been preserved through ages, of itself

no slight argument for its acceptance ; nor, again, on the grounds on which the Sacred Canon has been formed. The Canon has been taken as accepted ; the grounds for its acceptance have been stated satisfactorily by successive writers.

Taking Scripture as we receive it, our sole inquiry has been—How comes it that this Volume in our hands has marked its progress through the world with such emphasis ? what does it say of itself, and what does that account mean ?

CHAPTER XII.

INSPIRATION TO BE EXPECTED.

Inspiration a thing reasonably to be expected—Its acceptance will depend on state of Christian belief for time being.

A FEW remarks may close the whole.

It may be assumed that this whole world is the work of a Supreme Intelligent Being. We may assume this as proved to us by the argument from design and from final causes. Now, as no intelligent man is indifferent to the work of his hands, it cannot be supposed that the Author of all intelligence is indifferent to His work.

So also, every intelligent maker of a machine contrives it for a purpose, and the more intricate the mechanism, the more persistently will he be considered to have had his purpose in view; its success gladdens him, its failure is a cause of vexation.

The Great Maker of the universe must have had a purpose in view in our creation, must feel pleasure in the accomplishment of the purpose, or disappointed (if the term may be allowed) at our failure.

F

But how are men to know that purpose ?

The knowledge must be imparted by the Creator to the creatures of His hands. Yet everything the Creator does is by means ; if not visible Himself, He must work by instruments. He worketh hitherto in the sustentation of the world by instruments, although, from the regularity of His work, the perverse mind will sometimes dwell on the secondary as if it were the primary or originating cause. By instruments must He make known His will to His creatures, if they are to effect the purpose of their creation. There could be no other instrument so fitting as men themselves ; chosen by the Divine mind for the purpose, and yet distinctly understanding, and their hearers distinctly understanding, that the voice that speaks to them is from God.

And this is the whole theory of inspiration ; it should commend itself to a fair mind as forcibly as the conviction that all things spring from and are controlled by a Great First Cause.

The weight to be attached to inspiration, the reverence for the books which its influence is said to pervade, will rise or fall with the purity or the grossness of the Church of Christ, their keeper. When the love of purity and the zeal for truth die, or are at least on the wane, and the God that made and redeemed men is counted an intruder on their joys, then the Sacred Books sink in estimation, and are treated as ' devised fables,' and not even ' cunningly devised.'

When a young student of Divinity hears the Bible, which he has been taught from his childhood to hold in reverence, put on the level of a Latin Grammar and pulled to pieces as a Latin Grammar, let not his heart be dismayed. The same thing has occurred over and over again in the history of the Church of God, and yet the oracles of God have survived. They will survive still. For the opponent of inspiration, as of all miraculous agency, is in this dilemma : viz. that by upsetting or stamping out one difficulty, he involves himself in a greater. As I sit writing now, there is a void space between me and the wall of my room. It is a hard thing for me to believe that all at once a solid mass should arise in that void by, as Scripture here affirms, a Creator's hands. Yet it is a harder thing still to believe that such a solid mass could arise without any agent. I believe the received account of a Great First Cause as the more credible of the two.

It will be with inspiration as it has ever been with the Sacraments of Christ.

When His faith dies and His love waxes cold,

then the baptismal covenant becomes degraded to the mere giving a name, an outward form and no more, and the Eucharist sinks into an indifferent ceremony. When faith revives and the Spirit of God breathes again on the dry bones and gives them life, then the sacred records become treated with solemn awe, as the Visions of the Son of Man. It will be for the instruments who by their profession are called upon to feed the Church of God, to show that the storehouse of their food is the inexhaustible treasure-house of God.

www.ingramcontent.com/pod-product-compliance
Lightning Source LLC
Chambersburg PA
CBHW020338090426
42735CB00009B/1590